THE SUNSHINE

OF THE
MORNING

poetry by
Kirah West

The Sunshine of the Morning

LCCN: 2025922863

ISBN: 9798218843694

Printed in the United States of America.

Cover design by Kirah West © 2025

10 9 8 7 6 5 4 3 2 1

Preface

This collection is dedicated to all those who have fought silent battles,
endured pain beneath a hummed song, and conquered crippling fear
without the encouragement of others.
It is for the people you and I have never heard of,
never known, and may never meet.

This book exists for the people captured in these photographs, for
those behind the camera, and for the forgotten objects
gathering dust in the corners of antique stores-
items that may once have belonged to someone much like you.

My life has always felt like a fading memory.
I have tried so hard to become something I am not,
only to realize that I simply need to be myself.
In embracing my true self, I hope to honor the memory
of those who have come before us-
a sober reminder of the fleeting.
Perhaps, by living our own truths and waging the quiet war
against self-doubt, we carry forward the dreams
of those who never had the chance to realize theirs.

So, I present to you *The Sunshine of the Morning.*
It is honest, unvarnished, and strange,
much like the lives we try so hard to escape.
I hope the pages shine a light upon you, reminding you to reclaim
what has been pushed aside, and to remember the dreams
you were told to forget.

To my dear African American, Native American, Hispanic, Jewish, and readers of any racial minority:

I want you to know that your cultures, histories, and experiences matter immensely to me. The vintage images in this book are included solely for their aesthetic and symbolic context, not to exclude or overlook the invaluable contributions, struggles, or presence of people of color and other minorities.

Sadly, the photographs I've collected over the years (primarily from my upbringing in Midwestern Missouri) reflect the limited and often exclusionary lens of American history. The lack of minority representation in these images is a reflection of that history, not of my values or intentions.
Being someone who has experienced discrimination as a Jewish person, I understand the pain of erasure and exclusion, and I never want to perpetuate that.

Please know that these images are meant to evoke a sense of time and memory, not to endorse or romanticize a past that was unjust to so many. Your stories, your presence, and your representation are important to me— *then, now, and always.* You are welcome and safe here.

It is my sincere hope to find and include more diverse photographs for future works, as every story about people and the past should honor the full spectrum of humanity. Thank you for your understanding, and for being part of this journey with me.

With love and respect,
Kirah W.

To my younger self,
you were always worth it.

Part 1

Weak and resistless,

ignorant of tempestuous wrongdoing.

It is a cruel thing

how we are all born innocent,

even the most evil of people

in all ignoble history.

What slumping clay

we are to begin with,

how vast our void of knowledge,

and how eager the world be

to fill it.

What would it be

if you could know me

by what cannot be seen,

what I truly am.

The confidence I have

when I achieve with a purpose.

The excitement I feel,

the anticipation I possess.

The happiness I have

when all seems secure,

and the hope I carry

at the hearing of cure.

The rhythm that flows

when I am fast asleep,

the silent song

while my soul quietly weeps.

How my eyes light up

when I talk about something I love.

What if I were defined

by the things I actually am,

not what you might see.

What if I could be loved for me,

rather than what

I am expected to be?

I think the heart has an exterior skin
useless to the vessel
swelling underneath
and numbing to the possessor.

Perhaps, it is formed by a first rejection,
scarring like the dreams after war.

Although it may protect
the raw portion inside,
a casket's darkness
is the only home it provides.

Very few of us remember
what we existed as
when only unknowing we were,
before society demanded what we had to be,
when fending for ourselves
was never as important
as helping another
human being.

The skies are full of hope

you once had in younger days,

angels usher them in

and kiss their heads without shame.

The cry you utter

in the middle of the night

is what the stars weep for

as they dissipate into daylight.

Please,

do not be deceived

by the culmination

of these harrowing days;

the dreams you have forgotten

still caress your face

while in flight

years away.

I am nothing more
than a speck of dust,
empty with an airy core
of unworthy desires.
I am nothing less
than a brittle structure
of which my own hands and feet will crumble.
I scream,

    "Look! Pity at my hurt!"
   only to receive a silent breeze.

Foolish is the piece
of engorged ignorance
I call brain,
and arrogant the heart
I thought to be good.

I haven't any direction
for the task I have been assigned.
I've been trying to go home
                              my entire life.

Wherever a place beams of comfort
I have yet to dwell therein;
I've taken so many pieces
and tried to make them fit in.

There is just no explaining
that I really don't belong.
There's no nice way of putting it,
everyone seems to,
except for me,
move along.

I don't try to victimize
my existence,
for others have much worse fates,
but it does become
incredibly infuriating
to pretend I don't want a slice
of what everyone else
has heaped on their plates.

There is an old road behind an overgrown field,
  a few miles from the roaring of a highway,
    in-between the rotting trees an old barn sits forlornly.

I have driven past its barely-standing shafts of red,
but in my dreams I stepped inside and smelled a scent
of what was once alive, yet now has left a molded dust astride.

  A young man with hopes for affection
   left his poetry beneath the hay;
        an elderly pair whose lasting romance
          stays carved in the split of a door frame;
      a little girl who used to play
      tied strings along a creaking loft ladder;

and in that dark, rotting space
I found my heart silent and somber.

        What remains of their days?
        Will anyone remember their names?
        Can anyone know what they longed for,
          but could never come to see?

I awoke and still wonder
how people move on so quickly,
not reminded that remembered
is what everyone wants to be.

When the mirror looks back at you
it shows you an untrue self
in a colorless state.

You do not see the smiles
you have put on others faces.
You do not see the hope you
have given to those ready to quit.
You do not see the tears
you survived the night before,
or the strength it took
to make it this far.

You see a shell that exists
to be broken,
and although, most shells
are innately pretty-
no regard the size or color,
they have little way of proving
the belief, the will, the wonder.

Why do you say
I must die
without my mother?

Whose hand will I hold
as my soul begins to shutter?

She was the one who brought me up
and the one who stayed,
she has wrung my stomach
with a wretched ache-
her mortal, fleeing way.

(Needless to prove)
I need her.
I know I cannot forever soothe,
and when I am frail,
and cold,
and going;
tell me why my mother
is not there
to see me go
beyond the grave.

                I am certain she grieves the way I do,
            wishing she had a mother to see her through.

The best of fathers
could never replace
a mothers all-encompassing embrace.

That is how I know
God is awfully cruel:
to tell a child to grow taller
and be buried beneath the dirt
without the sound
of their mother's voice
helping them into the ground
before they perish
into the Earth.

We love the smell of rain,
  yet want it to leave.
We desire the sun,
  without stifling heat.

We always want the red
of a rose,
without the sting
  from its thorn.
We have never known happiness
  since the day we were born.

I miss our talks,

and the way you laughed with me.

The stupid things, (joking about)

no other mind could see.

There will not be a day

where I won't wander

throughout you,

or sit in tears pondering what you do.

I am still fixated

on all the dreams you had;

the lies I cradled in belief.

Your passionate speech.

The success you would so freely grab.

I know we had to part

because your love for me was not,

but I still love you

as much as the moment

I lay my eyes on your smiling face,

and my heart bore an ache

with precious thoughts

and a hopeful state.

Yellow

overcomes the fog below-

she sleeps

unaware of the haze,

for when she wakes

the world will be wrong,

but for now it is a hushing song.

Her scars look older

under the fading sun,

she will fight harder tomorrow

to prevent newer ones.

Death is an empty room

that calls her closer in,

but out the window

it's all mellow,

and she is still a child,

where anger temporarily retires.

Yellow is a mother

that always tried,

and a father

that never died.

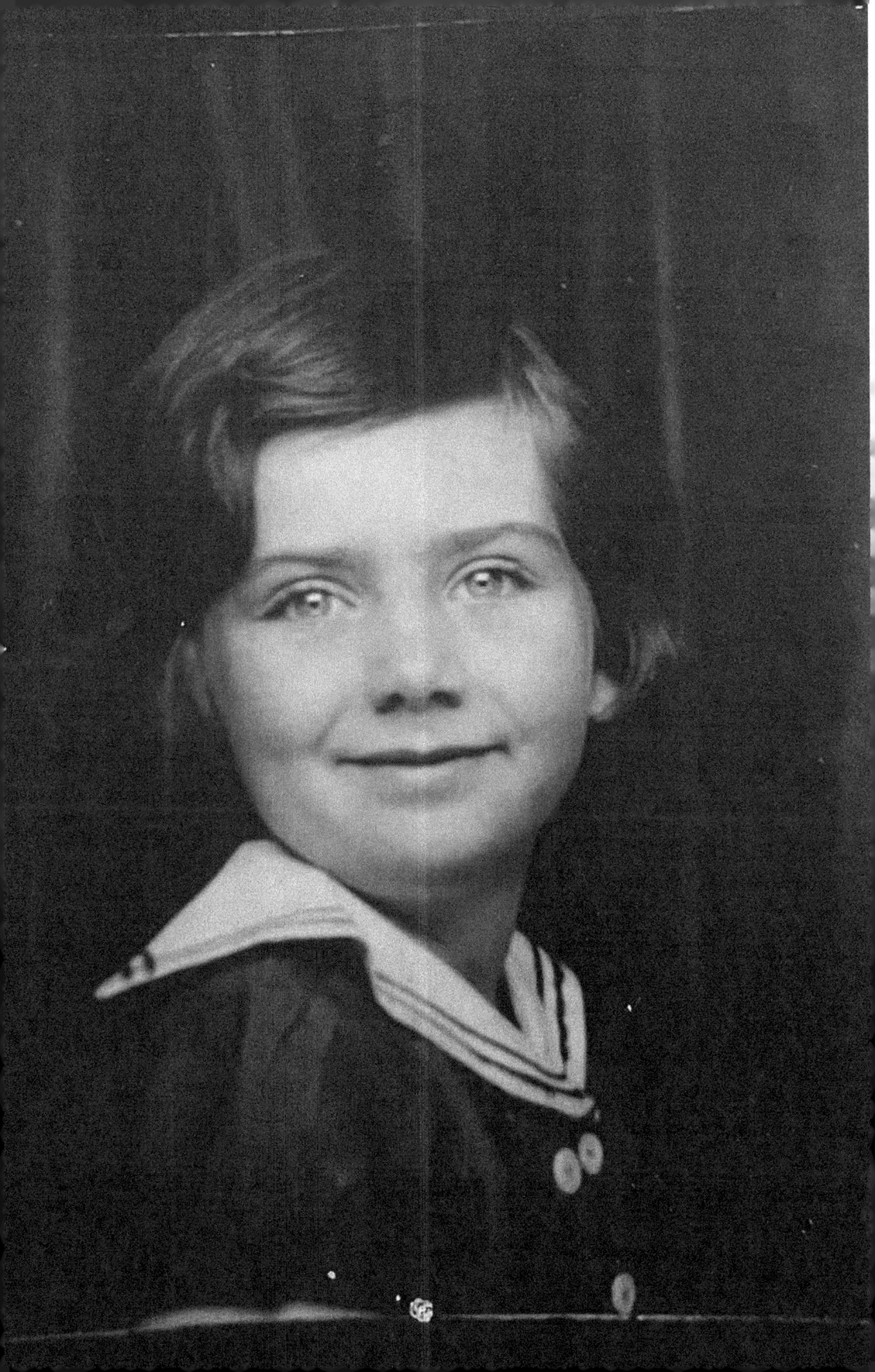

Sometimes,
the most heartfelt
and beautiful things
are not poetic.

They do not induce transcendence
with a hold slow
and meek.

They are tragically mundane
as rain on a fresh grave
that must be swiftly absorbed.

December is a tired woman
pushed to serve a cause
she does not believe in,
laboring for a worldly want,
passively asking for applause.

December is a cold hearted woman
who once might have been warm;
the salt in her wounds were praised
by those who wanted her gone.

December is a lonely woman
kept only for what she was born with,
the cheering for a new year
only makes her neck stiff.

You cannot name a human,

   for we are too horizonless to be summed.

Nothing abides within nothing,

you call it by title- it shudders

back to the shadows.

Label God and the skies;

   they only exist for themselves.

For the divine will not cease to be all they are

when lips dance a song of thought.

Souls cannot be given a price,

nor a textbook definition.

Never be sure to know for certain

   as the world is ever-changing

without a lyric, or suspicion.

                  Call out what?

   You know not of one's nature.

   Only feel what is already owned,

   and gratitude will be yours for the taking.

Meaning was never a linguistic classification,

but an explanatory undertaking

with no obligation for justification.

I saw you in the everyday
and I felt you in everything-
the warmth of my coat
while the snow bled
upon my face.

You lived in my nervous thoughts,
in the soreness of my head
as I let down my hair.

My body still burned in
the places you touched,
and my hand still held yours
although you held another.

You were with me each day,
but I never saw you again.

I find that I am content
just to be alive.
I'm happy to hear notes of music
and to feel the breeze of day.

Living is a privilege
(not given to all)
and I cherish every moment
knowing it may someday pass
as leaves during fall.

Every morning is sweet fruit
and solemn skies weep for me,
and I am here to behold
this greatness- what a blessed creature I be.

I still hear courage
in everything that breathes
and all the mysteries
of the Earth
are not as vivid as my love
for everything I see.

I cannot relate,

I never did,

I'll never understand

your capitalistic metropolis.

All you care for

is your valuable paper,

and your shallow careers,

the body you will marry,

and the meaningless affairs.

Every one of you is concerned

with who said something

which does not concern you,

and I merely exist

to sleep it through.

You care about the flow of your hair,

and the color of your face,

and I am lucky to care

about what I wear when I wake.

I don't find interest

in your obsession for status, or fame;

You are all strange to me,

and I don't want to play

an unwinnable game.

The damage is done,
under the rising sun
all is fair
as none is fair
for a world
forsaken and bare.

It is too late
to promise hope
to those who have been dragged
in the dirt
and the reality
of what they feared
they could not face.

The darkness has come,
cracking the surface
and the light shines through.
The aftermath of hell
glistens the way emeralds do.

The damage is done,
corpses decay as clouds roll on,
grimace if you must,
but remember now
that this is the truth
as it has always been,
and everyone has a sad story-
everyone has an end.

The darker times of life

are hunched over.

A timeworn man.

They praise success

while wanting it to end.

The ordinary problem,

the inevitable

no one wants to face.

The truth that we all are dying

at the same pace.

The wealthy and the beggar,

after coins they chase;

there is no difference to their ways.

We all seek to avoid pain

while it pools amidst our feet as we strain.

There is no cure

for the illness of hate,

as we know,

God seldom lets anyone in,

unless they were

somehow special to Him.

We have our opinions,

as past lives did then,

and whatever remains is

the dread they left therein.

The bottom of a bottle
was a solace
as I went ignoring
how betrayed I felt,
having known you were
with someone else.

My throat fills with
hot sand
each time I picture
the two of you
hand-in-hand.
You mind is a twisted storm
and my curiosity caused me
to reach within
melting into your undesirable hell
I never wanted to burn in.

My newborn daughter
is an old woman.
I sit her on my lap
and hold her withered hands.
Her eyes are glazed
from years before,
she has lived many lives.
I put her head to my chest
remembering nights when it was only us-
when her tiny body fit inside mine.
Her grey strands are wet from my tears.
The sun accentuates the lines in her face,
and the fuzz on her cardigan.
Her mind is full of memories
I will never know.
I am still her whole world
even after all the passing years.
She is still my sleepy-eyed,
crying baby that will always need my love.
I feel her tiring voice in my ear
as she reaches through time
to remind me
how precious it all is;
it is only us
and it always was,
always is.

I will come to *you* again

    when the leaves are

    seeping from your branches,

    the grass is glowing

    in your fields,

    the dew exudes in the

    humidity of your morning songs,

    and your wind blows against my skin

    like the touch of a child.

Then I will come to *you*,

and I will run to *you*,

and welcome *you*

    as I did two summers ago

    when all hope was lost,

    and joy was barely

    a dream.

Putting the past behind me
was one of the hardest things
I have had to do;
my heart thought memories
would always be true.
(As it turns out,
all things must die)
As I get older they are coming to an end,
they are fading as stars behind a sunrise.
It is not easy knowing now
I went my whole life wanting
something you could not give,
yet I have spent my days
amongst a ghost that whispers

> *"Fate deals equally unto all,*
> *no matter how hard the fall."*

Now, I am here in a sad
and new phase of being,
I am learning to accept
what I knew would come,
although, its truth
I could never sing.

It is winter's wrath
and the mercy of spring,
and whatever else happens in-between.

I would love to die
in an early summer glow,
against the dew
that settles as snow.

I think as I passed
into nothingness then
I would watch birds fly
throughout the hills
just above the horizon.
Perhaps I would not anguish,
no tears would I supply
for a foolish, human chant
that most offer as their
last goodbye.

I believe I would laugh
in a lowly sort of way
while I drifted into death
which turned out to be
just another tomorrow,
just another today.

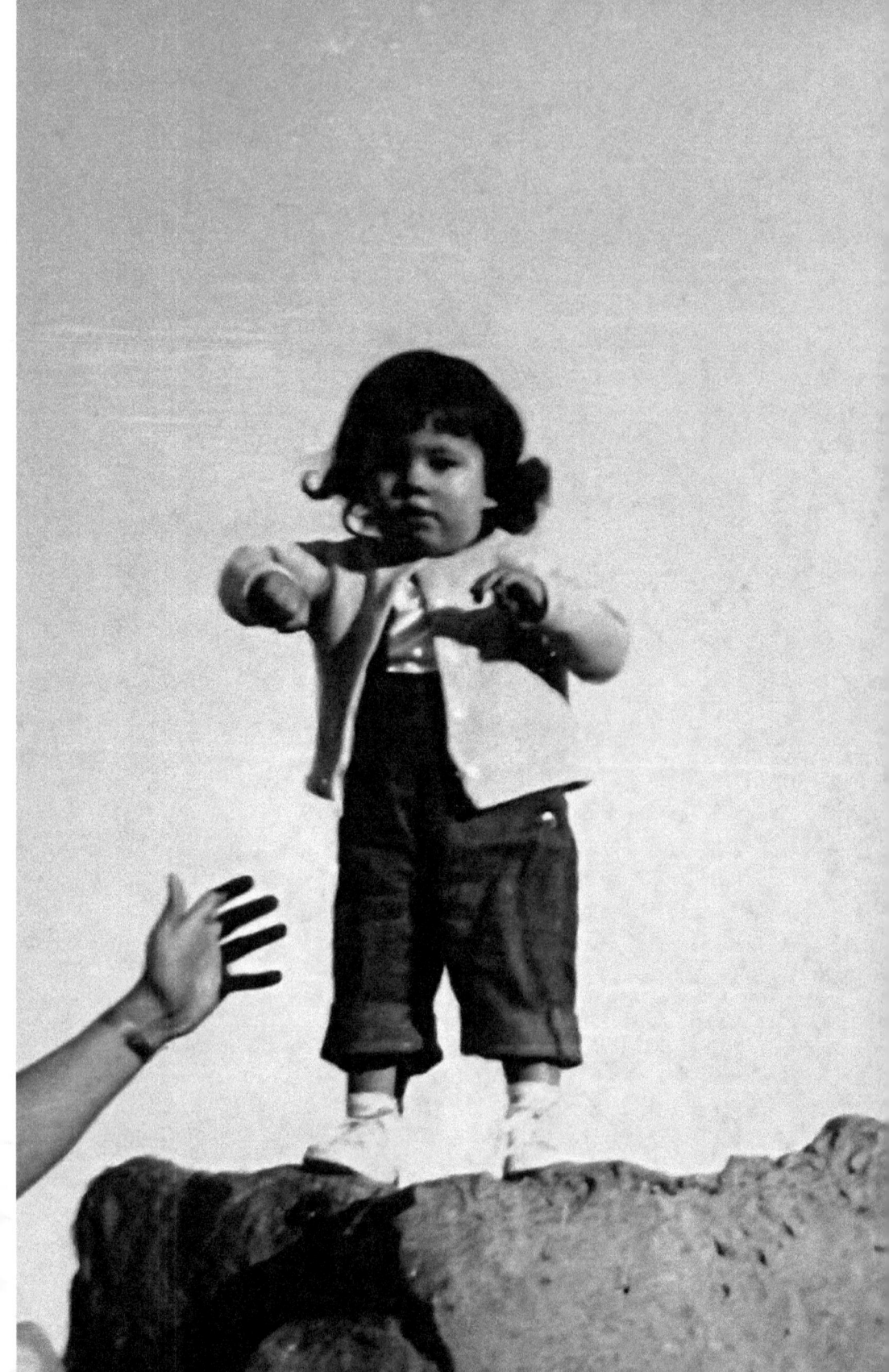

Am I good at anything?
Am I bad at everything?
Why can I not choose what to do
with a life I have claimed
to not care for or cling to?
Shouldn't there be an obvious plot
to the story walking me to the grave?

I love to sing and perform,
but I am too fat and my voice cracks;
I'd be laughed at.
I could invent and build with power,
but I am not good at math
and my ideas aren't original enough for that.
I am really not very good at anything.

Am I afraid of success?
Is it the way I look in a dress
that keeps me from being the best?

My IQ may be low,
my standards much lower;
the child within me
is still sobbing over the things she cannot control-
loathing herself for what she isn't,
and blaming God for what she is.
I'm only good at existing
and knowing what I won't do,
yet knowing what I wish to be
and keeping my self-esteem misconstrued.

I wished for you

the way children wish

to be seen.

I held onto you

as if you were

the only shining thing

I'd witnessed beam.

You knew I was unaware

of your youthful schemes,

and you were right, my darling,

because all the time that to her

you had been clinging

  I was alone in my bed

waiting for your call to ring.

He asked me about who I was.

  I told him how I loved

  vast, empty fields

  and forgotten towns with abandoned houses.

  Nostalgic notions that keep you up at night.

  I told him I loved hills at sunrise,

  the ones that go on past the morning clouds.

I ceased speaking

and started to dance,

but he told me he could not hear the music.

I showed him who I am,

and not what I did,

or what he thought I should be;

                    Then he left,

        and you'll find it often happens

        because people want to love our appearance

        and our selflessness.

I would rather be loved

for what my soul is made of,

and what my heart needs to thrive,

(maybe to breathe)

perhaps, to survive.

I lost all need for worldly gain,
I have no need for fleeting things.
I have been given a gift sweet and small;
all my heart can think
is how I will lose it all.
My joy is consistently captured by grief,
my mind remembers death. *(Away flies my peace)*
My eyes are swollen at the thought of life,
the shortening blur
of its narrowing sight
as it escapes like whispers
of the night.

> *How do I live here?*
> *How do I cope having this angel*
> *I will not long be able to hold?*
> *Will they ever know my love?*
> *What will be left of us?*

It is so difficult to accept
we must someday become
the haunting shadows
in forgotten depths
of what we wished
could last forever,
but know will vanish
with mortal breath.

Life was strange and hard for my heart,

    I could have never imagined how it tore me apart.

Now, you would think I suffered only in lies

    when you look at the happiness deep in my eyes.

It is such a dream far from yesterday,

    and there is nothing to grieve for today.

My soul is free in the fields of heaven-

    I understand all that kept me downtrodden.

It was not an end or a burden too heavy,

    it was not an evil master's game haunting me steadily.

I was drifting through a sea of doubtful sorrow

    and past the waves of circumstance

    I could not see the promised tomorrow.

All the people and places that vanished,

    the things I thought would seldom perish

    keep no grip upon me as they did then,

    and I realize they were stones in a stream

    I crossed once, never to cross again.

If you lay in endless resentment today,

    and wonder if your cares will forever keep you dismayed,

    know that once I was bound, not able to breathe,

    but now my feet dance along others who died before me.

It is wonderful and warm unlike the world you know,

    and everything has been set right;

    there is only peace and love has won the war.

So anguish not for your poorly hour on Earth,

    for they who will guide you through death

    has been with you ever since your birth.

When my daughter is of age
and life's toll is taking,
when she feels there's no happiness,
or purpose in the making,
perhaps, she reflects on years before.
Her own beauty she may fail to see;
it is then I will tell her what truth
I know to be:

When you were no taller than a rose stem
in a balmy spring day you sat amongst a field,
glowing in the wind.
While my heart was ever hopeless
from the pain and toil,
I watched you crumble leaves in your hands
as a god scatters stars.
Every morning you had a smile to greet me.
Some days were short, others long.
Your face never showed the dread I endured,
nor did your light ever dim in the shadows of my past.
For the moments I regretted breathing
you always kept me going
with the tear of your tiredness,
or your laugh at the world.
It was always you that got me through.
Now you may not feel it as the Earth is ever so dark,
but there was once a time
when you and I were never apart;
we spent early hours walking under the trees
and many afternoons I'd closely hold you
as you drifted into a nap time dream.
I held your body while it sobbed with sadness,
and I respected the roar of your anger,
and I never could have done anything greater.
For of all time, and of all men,
and of all things beyond our horizon,
I only ever wanted
my Carmen.

Did you for a while feel the way I did?
Could it be that you, for a moment,
   meant the things you said?

It was real to me,
it was always real to me.
As far as my eyes could see-
for I must have been blind with stupidity.
I don't think you were ever
secretly all the things I wanted you to be,
but I needed the comfort
so the weight of the pain
wouldn't destroy me.

For you, perhaps,
I was only a decal of inconvenience,
something to put up with,
but I woke wanting to see you-
I went to bed missing you.
The only man I felt safe around
until I was merely a noise in a city of sound.
I knew you had discarded others
before I was ever aware,

   but I was only a child,

and I couldn't see the truth
behind your absent-minded stare.

I should say I wish I never met you,
and provide all the harshness you deserve,
yet within, I am at peace with it all
even while it was not meant to last.
The facade you presented to me
was the love that I needed,
   the love that deserved to be true,
   the love I deserved to have.

When I was young

there was a window sealed with dust

where I watched the sun come up

over a hill of trees that caught the breeze,

(unbeknownst to me)

brought the sorrow of tomorrow.

Yesterday was precious

and I never knew it'd be a memory.

Land of yesterday,

you're too vivid in my mind;

(all the times we had

were never really mine).

When I was younger

I used to dream about the days to come,

now that I'm older

I'd rather, once again, be young.

Do you remember when life felt like a song?

The future reminds that life is a mess,

I guess it always was,

but I couldn't see past the bliss of innocence,

always wanting that sunrise to come;

now I'm lucky to reach night

without coming completely undone.

A tower that keeps getting hit

eventually must fall-

I wasn't ready to feel this small.

Yesterday was precious
and I never knew it'd be a memory.
Land of yesterday,
you're too vivid in my mind;
(all the times we had

were never really mine).
When I was younger
I used to dream about the days to come,
but these days
I'd rather, once again, be young.

Remember when a good day
gave you strength to carry on?
Now, I wish life were over with;
is this how humans make sense of philosophical conflict?
Writing meaningless poems
and pointless songs,
something to hum
while the wars wage on.

I was born at the end of August
when summer ends
and the sadness settles in;
a strange in-between
when leaves renew their promise
to die and come back as moments of next spring.

I've always been a wanderer,
the kind to lose their way,
and watch the stars fade
even past the nightmares
that plagued my days,
and caused an eternal heartache.

I've learned many a thing by this life,
I've watched people burning in blue flames
insist they're cold,
and I've seen the devil reach his hand,
and offer it to God as friends of old.

I'll never understand how to think,
or what to be sure of,
but I know the one rule
that always stays the same;
the dark of night will feel
like the end of everything
only to usher in
the sunshine of the morning.

I was born to an angry son of a dead father;

he never knew love and so,

he never knew his daughters.

I hold my mother in my arms

because I know she needs a mother,

and not a child to raise.

I've been burdened with the need

to comfort those who smile

as they silently bleed.

I've learned many a thing by this life,

I've seen my sister's fear

hide behind a joke in hope

I would hear laughter instead of a fight.

I've seen my brother run ever free

through fields of green and clouds of gold;

he'll never know of the pain set to unfold,

and today this is the peace

and the arm onto which I hold.

I'll never understand how to think

or what to be sure of,

but I know the one rule

that always stays the same;

the dark of night will feel

like the end of everything

only to usher in

the sunshine of the morning.

They say its heaven together
to live a wonderful life,
but when I look in your eyes
I see past humanity's height.

I want to die with you,
(lie in the fires with you)
as we fail to breath past the smoke,
for passing on holds a more sacred hope.
I long for the romance of having left-
messy and beautifully out of breath
while others behind exist within the war
and the aftermath,
our love grows stronger in death.

They say flesh is a desirable thing,
to die is to lose and to mourn,
but when you put your arms around me
I see bones entangled deep underneath.

I want to die with you
(lie in the fires with you)
as we fail to breath past the smoke,
for passing on holds a more sacred hope.
I long for the romance of having left-
messy and beautifully out of breath
while others behind exist within the war
and the aftermath,
our love grows stronger in death.

I've always longed for something
beyond the grave,
I knew you'd understand
the loneliness of my pain.
We belong to a passion
which lies at the end of our days,
and I live every hour
as if the world were ending today.

I want to die with you,
(lie under skies with you)
as we fail to breath past the smoke,
for passing on holds more sacred hope.
I long for the romance of having left-
messy and beautifully out of breath
while others behind exist within the war
and the aftermath,
our love grows stronger in death.

I took a drive the day I died
into the countryside.
I parked my car by a field.
I sunk into the seat and cried.

So much for a try,
wasted or passed by,
so meaningless the things
that took up time.

Down the road, into the beyond,
I remember how people endlessly fight
and riddle the days as they despond.
I wish I could go back
and tell them what all went wrong,
but I've already left the world
that with fraying strings
strums a song.

I got out of the car
and walked into the field.
I walked a little ways while the sky
faded from orange to dusty blue-
I think I faded too;
I couldn't feel the wind around me as it flew-
if they only knew.

So much for a life,
wasted, or passed by,
so meaningless the things
that took up my time.

Down the road, into the beyond,
I remember the people who fought just to hold on
and riddled the days that passed on.
I wish I could go back
and tell them what all went wrong,
but I've already left the world
that with broken bones
dances on.

Down the road, into the beyond,
I watch the people as they fight
and riddle the days that will soon be gone.
I wish I could go back
and tell them we are all wrong,
but I've already left the world
where useless ambition will forever prolong.

(It was never about right and wrong).

I don't wanna go back home,
I've traveled too far.
I've been gone too long
on some far off star.

I don't wanna leave
where the sky meets the sea.

What about the ones whose home
isn't so good?
How about the people
who can't live like they should?
Home is wherever you can escape
from the everyday hell-
if I could I'd cast a spell,
but all I've got are empty shells;
I think I am empty myself.

I don't wanna go back home,
I'm not ready to return.
My heart hurts too much to turn back
and I've learned what I had to learn.

Don't let me leave
where the sky meets the sea.

Let me run into the blue
where I might find peace.

Do you still have the card I sent?
Did you ever stop to think
maybe what I wrote
had a deeper intent?
Maybe I loved you-
was that what I meant?

And now, here I am,
missing someone I thought I knew
while you're fast asleep
with her in your bed;
   Happy Valentine's Day,
   Best regards to you.
(It's all about you)
I miss how it used to be
when I had two seconds of your time
and a lazy text to hang onto.

Do you remember
how at your feet I fell
with every thoughtless word you wrote?
I begged for the love
you never showed.

How could this be?
Did you want to hurt me?
Pushed my heart off the edge
when you ignored the sincere words I said.
Why did you request my company
when you had her instead?

And now, here I am,
missing someone I thought I knew
while you're fast asleep
with her in your bed;
   Happy Valentine's Day,
   Best regards to you.
(It's all about you)
I miss how it used to be
when I had one
or two seconds of your time,
and an afterthought to cling to.

When I said you were a dream
did you think I lied?
I know we're far away,
but I felt closer to you
than whatever was by my side.
Now we're strangers,
perhaps, we always were.
Your meaningless jokes
were something
for my empty heart to hold onto;
I thought the wall I put up
wasn't too strong for you to break through.

And now, here I am,
missing someone I thought I knew
while you're fast asleep
with her in your bed-
(Another body, another head)
I wished you missed me.
Do you still have the card I sent?

   Best Regards.
   No such address.
   Cannot send.

I decided to leave **1952**
because everything about it
reminded me of you.
I packed my bags
and with tears streaming down
I headed to **1973**
where I found none of you
and all of me.

You promised me the world,
but you never showed up at my door.
You gave me competition,
but I don't wanna keep a score.
I don't wanna have to go,
you keep looking her way-
I'll move on to another day
in another decade.

I could have gone back to **1921**
and been a wiser one,
left way before you were dead,
but I am meant to run ahead,
not stagger far behind
as you did every single time.

I guess it was just pretend
and I was never meant for you,
but I still dream about the days
we spent together in **1952.**

These shoes are wearing out
from all our mindless walks
and I unplug the phone
before you call to talk.
I don't wanna have to go,
but you keep looking her way-
I'll move on to another day
in another decade.

We don't belong together.
   Our magic moments
ran out of tricks for the stage-
   moon river turned out
to be a two-way stream.
Honey, sometimes I wish
you would've stayed true to me.

I tried to love you, dear,
but you always left me behind;
you don't deserve
the kind of love I give.
You're so blind.

I'll always love you
even though you wont give me
a second thought.
I don't wanna have to go,
but you keep looking her way,
so I'll move on to another day
in another decade.

Part 2

The truth is

I stopped dreaming;

I have dug myself out of the pit.

I have faced the sunshine,

and my mind

and my heart

have simply no idea how to stay

under the warmth

when I have done nothing

but imagine how it would feel

while in the cold.

I am feeling the strain of life tonight,
I am understanding more about it
during the trouble when nothing is right.

I am learning how every person
lives an existence brief,
    and how each moment is a treasure to keep.
        It is all a whirlwind,
        it flies by, the good and the bad.
        Every song, every tragedy, every chance,
        every fenced-in field I pass;
        all of what seems quiet, but is present,
        and ready to be marveled at.

        I am seeing how delicate it all is,
        the weight of what each story means-
        to every ember of violence,
        to the scent that lures the bee.

Someone watches in their own quiet way,
and reaches down to guide us every day.

    It is as if we cannot be happy,
    it is almost as if we do not care
    how this fleeting promise of life
                we are given
        will someday pass away
        into thin air.

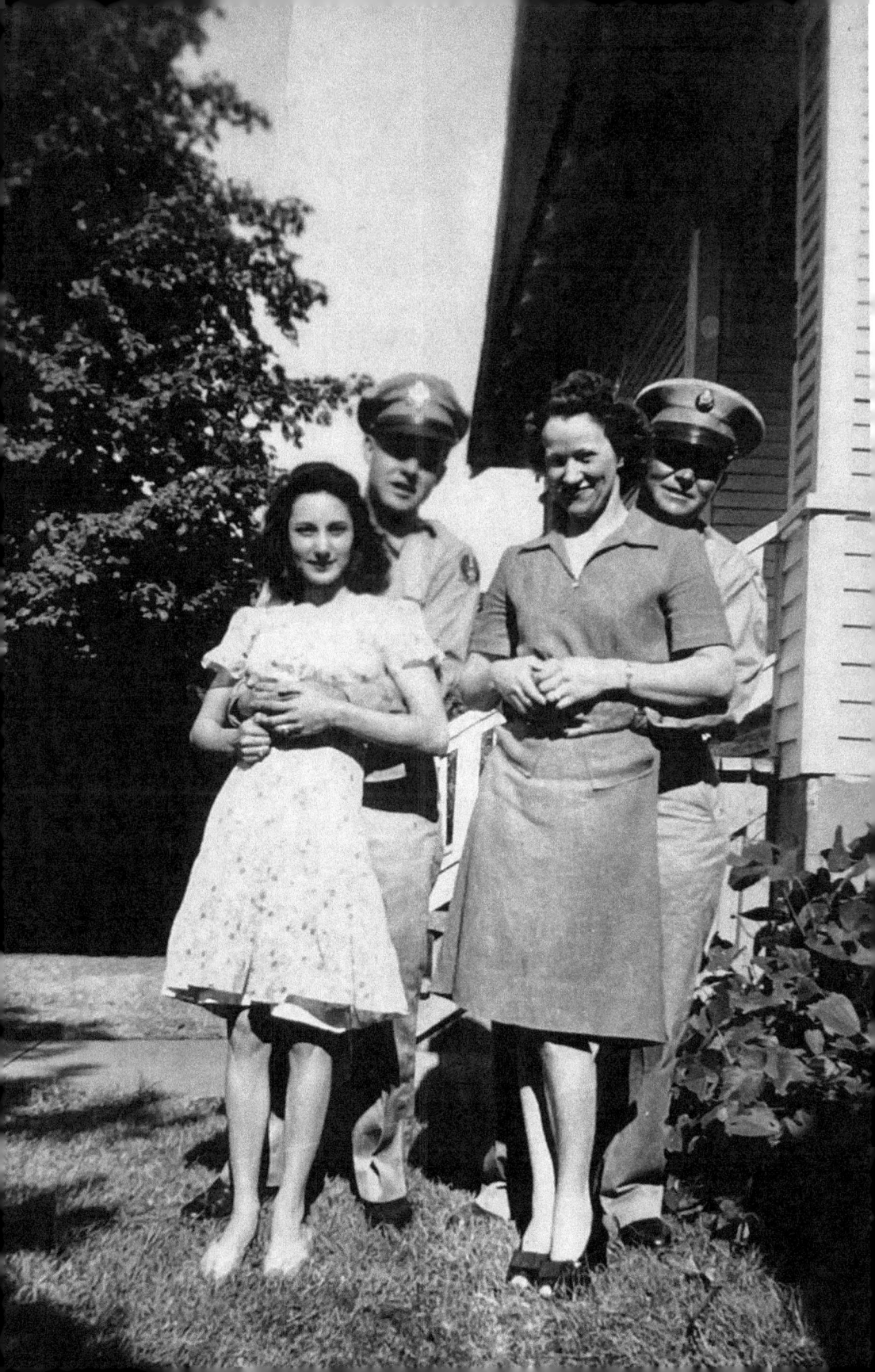

You died so long ago.

Your spirit left

leaving my heart broken in two,

of course, I held onto you;

it's all I knew how to do.

Your breathless figure bare before me,

rotting so eyes could see.

Rooms of my mind claimed the stench of death,

but I swore I would keep you with me

long after your last breath.

I loved you though you were no longer here.

Your skin; a sunken display,

highlights the memories I held dear.

I didn't care about the way you lay still,

I did everything for you.

I lived for something deceased

when my heart was beating ready, and real.

I got used to you having passed away

that I mistook you for someone moving today.

Each morning, I awake

to your expressionless face

staring back at me in our crumbling bed.

I always wished you would answer me

when I spoke, but you remained quiet

and added to my dread.

Will I ever let go of you?

Will this haunted house ever see new life,

or will my fate be to embrace the dead

as they decay in my sight?

I found God today,
I found them in the moments
I wanted to leave,
but decided to stay.

I found them when I was sore with a wound,
not when I was smiling or soothed.

The only time I have ever seen their face
was when I looked upon my own with disgrace.

I've never been closer to God in my life
than when depression ruled my days
and madness overtook my mind.

There is a forgotten child
that awaits at the gate
between life and death,
and they never grin
or carelessly jest.
They are God,
along with all the rest
who never had a chance-
whose poorly fate was always
their promised best.

I took a picture of a flower
in a place I seldom go,
its hue lured my sight
many years ago.

I thought about going again
to see if it still blooms.
I know it is silly
to think it would
as things pass on
while winter consumes.

If I found another plant
that looked as beautiful as it,
and I told it my stories
and my fears,
would it also understand
the way the other one did?

I know I am a fool
for wishing life to stay the same,
yet, as death draws nearer
I find myself
wanting to relive older days,
and the moments that fled
as quickly as they came.

In another life
my father loves me;
my father loves my mother
and only uses his hands
to hold her face.
We eat together,
we laugh
and he wipes crumbs
off my shirt.
Everything is simple
and I am only a girl to him,
only a child.
I sit on his lap
and he sees only a baby,
only feels my smile,
and I am safe.
He wishes to love what he created,
he never wishes a harmful thing.
His only aggression is in play
and he is there to stay.
I do not fear him,
our sun is so bright,
and the day ahead is something
I will not have to fight.
My father loves me,
I am alright
in another life.

I've found it hard not to tell

of what my heart was trying,

I am often not keen to let uncertainty

go on emphasizing.

Yet, I could not help

but take a moment to say

all the things I've been thinking,

or at least a small attempt to portray

what I have hidden in my heart for you

from our first day.

Life has been hard,

(but with *you* less harder).

I have had my doubts,

but your love was always larger.

        Oftentimes, I feel life is only sorrowful,

        and everything is rushing by,

        yet, when I am holding your hand

        it is as slow and peaceful as the sky.

          I do not know what I did that grasped your attention,

                  I am not sure what I could have done

                        to gain your affection,

             but I find myself lost in a realm of hope

             even when the world is a harrowing slope.

I always dreamed of knowing love with a fearless gaze

as my whole life has seemed an endless maze—

whatever happens, I hope you always know

you were my only lover, my first choice;

if we are side by side,

I can face tomorrow.

Some of us are waiting
to watch it all
come crashing down.
We know life
never gets better,
We know our eternity
doesn't give in the end.
Some of us
have already tried,
we gave up long before
you ever believed.
We are watching
the whale fall,
ready to drown
in the depths below.
Whatever will be
is all there is,
we didn't ask to live.
Acceptance is bitter,
but denial is merely worthless.

I think heaven is a wildflower
most trample or pass by.
Maybe it's out in a pasture
where people rarely set foot,
but many drive by.
Perhaps, it hears doves cry,
and feels the brush of a creature
now and then.
Maybe insects crawl along its weak stem.
What happens, I wonder, when it dies?
   Does heaven cease to exist for a while
   and regrow later in time?
If it's eaten along a rabbits graze,
   does heaven live in its heart
   and resound in its squeak?
What if it is never touched, nor seen?
   Is heaven somewhere waiting to be found,
   or can it be found at all?
If I made a heaven, I'd hide it in a flower
where no one could see,
that way I'd know it'd be safe
for those who are truly in need,
or I'd let it pass away
to help grow new life
for next spring.

Love you forever

although we are apart.

Love you for always

even while our nearness is not.

Love you forever, my darling,

you will be alright;

loving forever

just wasn't meant

for us tonight.

You were born,
you took your first breath of air
   and that was enough.
You cried in need
and laughed in confidence,
   and that was as heaven.
To see and to taste,
to feel and to hear,
to behold the world,
   to be really human.
To love and to be loved.
To be caressed by wind.
The sober when freezing
and the lull of warmth.
To eat and feel full.
To read and remember what you have read.
To become upset and to be calm,
to learn the misunderstood,
or to comprehend all too well.
To serve and assist,
to crave and to yearn.
To be without obligation
or extraordinary expectation.
No need to be grand,
no need to be known by the world,
and no need to be magnificent.
There is no pressure to be anything
but yourself,
   because that is enough,
   it has always been enough
   since the very beginning.

I weep tears

and streams are formed in forests.

I cut my skin

and the ground becomes unsewn.

I am a part of this earth

and I feel every step

and I feel every prayer

the trees have sung.

He said to me,

*"The sun rises
and you wake,
but the night
comes to satisfy
and sate."*

I said to him,

"I breathe, therefore, I live."

He uttered out to me,

*"You breathe,
therefore, you exist,
you dream,
therefore, you live."*

I laughed,

and God came as the Sun

shining gently through the thick

of the fog

and lasting until the day was done.

I wept,

and God came as wind

drying my tear stained face

and comforting my shaking hands.

I fell to death,

and the moment I could not see,

God came as a mother

and cradled me.

Let yourself be exquisitely alive.
Rid of your need for customs,
live as the truer you,
and burn for your life.

Do not live for money,
(it will be saved and spent just the same).

Do not live for appearance,
(the earth will not critique your body as it decays).

Do not live for pleasure,
(it will end as quickly as it began).

Do not live for friends,
(people move on).

Do not live for fame,
(your death is the only thing promised to you).

What if you ceased
from whining for yourself?

This is the future
and today is already tomorrow.

Isn't it marvelous?
At any time, at any place,
you can allow yourself to be happy-
like the swift snap of a twig,
or the breakage of heat
when a breeze passes by the skin.
  Just so,
you have permission
to be altogether joyful in heart
which is hope despite the circumstances.
.

If the one who seeks light wishes to see,

does the one who seeks night

wish to be blind?

I have always loved to search out

what everyone else ignores-

what has been left behind;

there must be a reason

why they overlook it.

I relate to the voiceless things,

the grimy objects lodged in corners.

I see myself

in the eyes of a child

in a past-time photograph.

I feel their stories

and I hear their grief.

    I am in love

    with all the forgotten things.

I took a walk in the woods
when my soul had fallen into despair,
I heard the flowers whisper
"She is not well, I fear."

I put my hands along the trees
to feel their humble smiles.
I felt their warmth embrace me
as I went on for miles.

I looked up to see a scattered green
falling all around the day.
I fell in love with everything
sprouting up beside the way.

I felt the wind begin to draw me
across the stream and farther in;
I looked back only once to say
"I must go, it's calling me in."

You have been strong;
you have stood and been brave
in the easiest of places to be fearful.

You have been the flower
that blooms by blood on the battlefield.

Doing the will *despite* the hardship.
Exercising aspiration for sake of overcoming doubt.

You do not pretend,
you do not give up,
you just keep going
because if you do not
you will die,
and you do not really want to die;
    you just want to stop hurting.

The rays of the Sun
are quite like you-
they come and go,
shining brighter
than anything
when they do.

Through it all
I find wisdom,
as it be
gracious enough to stay,
but smart enough to leave.

I am somewhere *far away,*
standing right outside a little house
with nothing to stress about
on the side of a hill looking out.
My hands are holding books
and I smell the scent of flowers
as I hear bells in a church tower.
Out there, I see peace
as sobering storms of faith,
there is no sense of refrain.
It causes my attention to look over
what exists right now
and in this dream
I seem to be alone,
but happy somehow-
nestled in a hillside
along a sparkling stream,
having songs to sing,
and doing things I love
without the competition
that only leaves you grieving.
Can happiness come
from simply being?

I feel like I am falling,
                       but I have never let go.
I sense I have been performing,
                       yet, there has been no applause for my show.
I know I have been hit,
                       though I see no bruise.
I am sure this circus of a life
                       is all I can look forward to.

Humans are the most lovely
and atrocious creatures
in the world.

It takes incredible love
to make sense
of entwining chaos.

I push the clock forward

twenty-four hours each day;

I cannot live in the current time.

I am always a day ahead,

counting my fingers to see

just how many days I can live

before this one is through.

I cannot exist as I should

because I am always wishing

I were with you.

There was something richer than wealth,
something larger than space,
and grander than heart.

There was a thought of freedom-
a realization of love
while she felt the weight
lift off her shoulders
like birds taking flight,
and in that moment
she felt the beauty of life.

"Are you an artist?"

                              "No, I lack the skill."

"Not in my opinion."

                                       "Oh?"

"You have created
something in me,
and now I am so many
different colors."

If I be ill,
I will happy to think of you.

If I be well,
I will be happy to hear your voice.

If I be alive for many days more,
I promise to love you
more than the day before.

When I die,
I know you will be there
to see my last breath
the moment before my death.

Little girls aren't meant
to devour their own hearts,
but that's what I did to survive-
    I fought.
Tiny hands shouldn't hold
the weight of a man.
Small shoes can only walk
in the footsteps
of where they've never been.
My body was a morgue
for all the secrets you hid from them,
and the more you fit inside
the faster my soul caved in.

Little girls are supposed to sing and play
innocence merely existing
as the dream of a new day,
but you turned me into a mewling lamb,
crying as the wolf broke the skin;
my mother was *too far* to hear me.

I was no longer a child,
I morphed into something
that follows as a dog would,
and when one reaches out to me
I only know to bare my teeth.
    (My leg is only halfway gnawed
    from the trap it is caught within).

Little girls are meant to be little
in a holy sort of way;
    am I the devil's daughter
    for enduring what makes no sense?
    Or for what I could have been
    if I had only been given the chance?

You kissed me with sugar,

you filled my wounds with salt,

and now my scars have crystallized.

My lips harbor still a dulcet taste.

  I would rather kiss another

  despite the bitter taste.

I held something precious in my hand-

I treasured it,

I cared for it,

I wrote it on my heart.

One day, I watched it bleed

and slip through my fingers.

Maybe the wind is magic
and every time it flows by you,
running through your hair,
it leaves a tiny trace-
an iridescent piece of heaven
inside you
although you are unaware.

I am lying in a splintered bed-
in a house of screams;
I am numb
to all the sound I hear.
My limbs have gone cold
and my head hollow.

    This is the epitome of torment,
    but it's poorly enough
    to minimize somehow;
    trying to sleep
    in the midst of flames
    that cannot ever
    burn out.

It's a funny thing,
you know,
how we are all trying
to be a stiff, iron statue-
a replica of the common sight
  rather than ourselves.

I find it amusing
we are all so moved
to be absolutely normal
when we could be
insanely interesting instead.

I find it odd that humans
do not believe in what
they cannot see
while feeling wind.

I wish the amount of times
people saw you
and thought you were *beautiful*
turned into telegrams
you would receive
each day;

I tell you,
they would span lifetimes.

I found you unforgettable

in all aspects,

your every word

was a line

in my mind's book,

and your every stare

started my hearts beat.

Your laugh supported

the walls of my lungs

and then you left,

leaving the air to flee

my rubbery body

and the love to leave

my dusty eyes.

There are those

who could live

      on every planet,

      spend every coin,

      and live every life,

but would choose

to stay the same;

they are the wisest

among us all.

The greater her adversity
the more splendid her spirit;
she will fly through debris
and smile in the face of torment.
She will stay though told to leave,
she will cry
while others are laughing,
but she will not abandon
her dearest love:
humanity.

The writer is a traveler
walking unknown roads,
winding up in the same end
they always come to,
yesterday-
  overmorrow.

They search
for a caving house
where they can hide,
a place they dare call home
if they could ever stay
  long enough to decide.

Maybe someday
their stories
for which they fight,
will take them to a place
  of which they write.

True prison has no walls,
or alarm to hinder escape;
it is the frame of mind
that always has an open door.

Many people are living
in their own cell
and with chattering teeth
are longing to run
while fidgeting with the key.

How vastly hypnotized
I have become
at this dreadful task
deemed living.

Let it be said
that a smile was never
so precious
as the one that swam
through tears;
Indeed,
it is my life
which knows it
to be true.

When I first met you

I could not tell

just how much in love

with you I fell.

What a dream you are

to a sad soul

with a sorry story to tell.

You removed the door to my heart,

kept my enemies far apart,

you took me to a place

deep in crowded woods

left inside my childhood-

hidden away where my fears lay

in the lost dreams of my stolen song.

It was in your eyes

all of life made sense,

it hurts to say farewell ever since

your hand ran through my hair,

and all my worries blended

with the balmy air.

   I am in love

   with the tomorrows

   you sell,

   they please

   and seduce me so well.

I know why people do not like God,
(I know why God does not exist)
I am certain of why He is unfair
and passive in His powerlessness.
Where God lives people see themselves
   as they truly are,
rather than what they ought to be.
Where kind men are cruel
and strong men are weak;
perhaps, everyone must work
and not wish for what they seek.

Heaven is all there is
because hell is far too strict
for people who are inherently cruel,
but not ever cruel enough for punishment.

You want the joy without the sorrow,
you want the privilege
without the loyalty;
you utter a prayer as a politician
would offer a speech.

I know why people do not like God,
He shows them the truth of their heart
they always considered honest and sweet
while it laughed in sin as it beat.

Is this living?

Is this life?

Is this the fate for which we were born and designed?

We are continuously forgotten in the tides of time.

Is there no hope for those who exist as waves

reaching high only to fall and die?

Will God help all the voices in the night?

Everyday is another fight to survive.

There is only death in death; inspiration is the work of the living.

Table of Contents

Kirah is an author, artist, and devoted mother whose work is fueled by a deep passion for feminism, spirituality, and advocacy for equality.

She penned her first poetry book at just nineteen, launching a literary journey defined by humble beginnings, raw emotion, and a compelling voice that stands apart in today's poetry market.